I'M CONFUSED ABOUT DATING

Joel James

Consulting Editor: Dr. Paul Tautges

Help! I'm Confused About Dating

© 2017 Joel James

ISBN
Paper: 978-1-63342-042-7
ePub: 978-1-63342-043-4
Mobi: 978-1-63342-044-1

Published by **Shepherd Press**
P.O. Box 24
Wapwallopen, PA 18660

www.shepherdpress.com

Scripture quotations are from the New American Standard Bible (The Lockman Foundation, 1995).

All rights reserved.

No part of this publication may be reproduced, or stored in a retrieval system, or transmitted, in any form or by any means, mechanical, electronic, photocopying, recording or otherwise, without the prior permission of Shepherd Press.

Designed by **documen**

Contents

	Introduction	5
1	Dating Don'ts	9
2	The Companionship Principle	15
3	Where, What, When, and Whom?	22
4	Purity and Dating	36
	Conclusion: Is This the One?	50
	Personal Application Projects	59
	Where Can I Get More Help?	62

Introduction

My dating experiences before I met and married my wife were not exactly the highlights of my youth. Take my first date, for example. Everything that could have gone wrong did.

I asked a lovely Christian girl named Julie to accompany me to a Christian concert, and she was kind enough to accept. When the afternoon of the concert came, Julie called to say that she was feeling ill, but that she still wanted to come. In fact, when she arrived at my dorm just before it was time to leave, she looked awful. Drawn, pale—she was clearly not in top form. I told her she didn't have to come, but she obviously felt that she had given her word and wanted to keep it. I'm sure she felt a lot better when we bumped into her former boyfriend on our way out of the building. I hate it when that happens.

Ready to depart, we got into my friend's car. I

Help! I'm Confused about Dating

didn't own a car and thought a 120-mile ride on the back of my bicycle might be a bit uncomfortable for her, so the five of us squeezed into my friend's vehicle: three guys, me, and Julie. Nice. Romantic. Immediately after we had loaded into the car, I unloaded. I had forgotten our tickets and had to go back to my dorm room to get them. Organized, that's me.

The concert was in another city about an hour away, and just before we arrived at the concert hall, my friend's car started to smoke slightly. We didn't think much of it; we were too eager to see the show.

Julie had tried her best to make small talk on the way, but she was clearly paddling upstream against a strong current. You can imagine how much better three hours of loud music made her feel. After the concert we piled back into my friend's car and started home. On the outskirts of the city where the concert was, the car blew up. The dashboard lights went berserk, smoke started rolling in through all the vents, and we had to pull over and stop.

While my friends went for help, I spent the next three-and-a-half hours watching Julie slowly freeze as the temperature plummeted. My only hope was that, if she got cold enough, she might forget how sick she was. In the end, it was after two in the morning by the time we got home.

Needless to say, we didn't go out again. In fact, Julie got married a short time later. One date with me was enough to convince her that she needed to take herself out of the field, and quickly.

Dating is crazy sometimes, isn't it? But, to be honest, car fires in the middle of the night are the least of it. The real reason dating is crazy is mainly because Christian young people and parents have never consciously shaped their understanding of dating by the Bible. In fact, dating is one of the most obvious areas where Christians have blindly followed the path beaten by the world. Paul told the church in Rome,

> Do not be conformed to this world.
> (Romans 12:2)

If ever there was an area where we need to resist being pressed into the world's mold, dating is it.

However, the Bible seems to have lost its voice when it comes to dating. Dating, as we practice it, simply isn't found in Scripture. The approach of God's people was very different. How different? When forty-year-old Isaac wanted to get married, he didn't borrow Dad's camel and take a girl to the movies. Instead his dad, Abraham, sent one of his trusted servants about five hundred miles away to Mesopotamia to pick a girl for Isaac, and she assented to the marriage without even meeting him (Genesis 24). That's different!

As a parent myself now, I'm beginning to think Abraham's approach wasn't such a bad idea. However, while the parental-appointment method is *described* in the Bible, it is never *prescribed* or commanded. Therefore, it is impossible to say that arranged marriages are the biblical method. If nothing else, the interaction between Ruth and Boaz in the book of Ruth shows that there was freedom in this area.

While we don't have the luxury of turning to *the* biblical passage on dating and reading God's final word on the subject, we do know that God's Word is sufficient for life and godliness (2 Peter 1:3). Therefore, the guidance we need regarding dating is there; we just need to find it.

1
Dating Don'ts

One way of learning how to do something is by watching someone else do it poorly. When I swam in triathlons, I had a friend who worked out in the same pool. In his freestyle stroke, he had a habit of putting his hand in the water too far toward the centerline of his body, turning his body slightly sideways. Therefore, instead of gliding through the water, he snow-plowed the water in front of him. I learned a lot by watching him: I learned how *not* to swim. His mistake helped me correct a similar error in my own stroke.

Perhaps we can use that same approach as we consider how Samson went about finding a wife. I once heard a dating talk entitled "The Dos and Don'ts of Dating." Unfortunately, in chapters 14–16 of the book of Judges, we find only the *don'ts* of dating. There are no *dos* in Samson's story. He did everything wrongly.

> Then Samson went down to Timnah
> and saw a woman in Timnah, one of

> *the daughters of the Philistines. So he came back and told his father and mother, "I saw a woman in Timnah, one of the daughters of the Philistines; now therefore, get her for me as a wife."*
>
> (Judges 14:1–2)

Samson had seen girls before, but this one was a real knockout. So much so, he immediately decided he wanted to marry her. What's wrong with that? Boy meets girl. Boy flips his lid. Boy asks girl to marry him. Love at first sight ... how romantic!

What was wrong with Samson's approach to dating? Everything. Specifically, he made three disastrous mistakes.

Don't #1

Samson was visiting Timnah and saw "one of the daughters of the Philistines." What was the problem with that? Just this: Israel had been commanded by God not to marry the daughters of the idolatrous, demon-worshipping peoples around them (Deuteronomy 7:3–4). It was a wise command. God didn't want his people being led astray by the idol worship and occult practices of the Canaanites, the Philistines, and others.

In other words, Samson had no business going to Timnah with a roving eye. Every girl there was off-limits. Unfortunately, Samson never learned his lesson. If it wasn't a sweetheart in Timnah, it was a prostitute in Gaza (Judges 16:1), and when he grew tired of her, he pursued yet another Philistine lover, the delectable Delilah (16:4). The land of the Philistines was the home of a wicked and immoral people, and every time Samson went there, his lust pulled him into another disastrous relationship.

Ignoring God's commands, Samson told his father, "Get her for me, for she looks good to me" (Judges 14:3). The original language actually says "She is *righteous* or *upright* to me." According to Samson, Miss Timnah met the accepted standard. Unfortunately, as a worshipper of the gods of the Philistines, she definitely did not meet God's standards. But Samson was adamant: "She meets the standard." When the girl Samson wanted didn't measure up, he changed the rules. Not even God's commands stopped him from pursuing the girl he desired.

Don't #2

Besides looking for love in all the wrong places, Samson had another major problem in his approach to dating. How did Samson determine that a girl would be a good partner? "I *saw* a woman in Timnah" (Judges 14:2, emphasis added). Samson's measure of a woman was her profile. Always the human hormone, Samson thought only of sex appeal when he searched for a wife. Her faith and her character were inconsequential. If the curve of her face and the cut of her hair were right, then it was full steam ahead.

Don't #3

> Then his father and his mother said to him, "Is there no woman among the daughters of your relatives, or among all our people, that you go to take a wife from the uncircumcised Philistines?" But Samson said to his father, "Get her for me, for she looks good to me."
>
> (Judges 14:3)

Proverbs says,

> *Foolishness is bound up in the heart of a child.*
>
> (Proverbs 22:15)

Certainly that was true of Samson. His parents tried to warn him. They strongly encouraged him to reconsider his course of action. Samson's response? "Dad, Mom, you're idiots. I know better than you do." Blinded by infatuation, Samson rejected his parents' counsel. In so doing, he steamrolled right over one of God's most important lines of defense protecting us against foolish decisions.

Pride Goes before Destruction

You probably know the rest of the story. Before the wedding feast was over, Samson's beautiful bride had manipulated and betrayed him. She nagged and whined out of him the answer to the riddle he had invented to stump her wedding guests (Judges 14:16–17). Samson left the wedding in a fury and stormed out of town. Eventually, after several bouts of revenge and counter-revenge between Samson and his wife's friends, Judges 15:8

tells us that Samson ended up living in a cave like an outlaw. His self-styled approach to dating didn't bring him the happiness and pleasure he thought it would. It brought only manipulation, distrust, faithlessness, in-law squabbles, anger, vengeance, and loneliness.

Samson was forever putting himself in situations where he could become emotionally and physically involved with an unbeliever. And, inevitably, he did. He also measured a prospective companion only by her physical attractiveness rather than by her love for God. And when his parents tried to shine the light of wisdom on his bad decision, he turned a blind eye to their counsel. Those are three classic blunders, and Samson made them all.

2
The Companionship Principle

The wreckage of Samson's marriage illustrates the importance of pursuing a husband or wife in a biblical manner. Having seen *how not* to do it, we must now consider *how* to do it. How can we bring biblical sanity to the insanity of dating?

At its most basic level, dating is a relationship between a man and a woman. The key verse in the Bible on such relationships is Genesis 2:18:

> Then the LORD God said, "It is not good for the man to be alone; I will make him a helper suitable for him."

According to this verse, God designed both loneliness and helplessness into the first man. No animal could satisfy Adam's desires for companionship; therefore, God created Eve. Although some people have been given the gift of being single and satisfied (1 Corinthians 7:7), the vast majority of us have Genesis 2:18 written on our hearts in day-glow ink. We are hardwired by God to desire a relationship of deep, intimate friendship with someone from the opposite sex.

In other words, dating exists because we desire a Genesis 2:18 *marriage-kind-of-relationship*. That doesn't mean that people always date because they want to get married. But it does mean that we date because God has built into us a desire for intimacy and companionship in a unique man/woman relationship. Understanding dating that way is significant. It tells us the goal of dating: the companionship of Genesis 2:18. If that's true, where do you think you should put your emphasis in dating? That's right: on friendship or companionship.

When I was at college, there was a girl in my church who was bright and attractive, and who genuinely loved Christ. As you can imagine, she was like a car radiator—the bugs were all over her. The pastor of our college group once made an interesting private comment about her. "Poor Jill," he said, "everybody wants to marry her, but nobody wants to take the time to be her friend first." That was an insightful comment from a man who understood what dating is about.

The foundation of a good marriage is a right relationship with God through Jesus Christ.

But following on the heels of that is a strong friendship. If you take away the romance, sex, children, and everything else we associate with marriage, if you still have a strong friendship, you still have a strong marriage. In other words, since dating (to some degree or another) is the pursuit of a marriage-kind-of-relationship, then everything you do in dating should be guided by *the companionship principle*.

As I look back at my single days, the few girls I was interested in all shared one characteristic besides a love for Christ. It wasn't their looks, education, or talents; it was that they all were easy to talk to. We had an easy, natural friendship. Without knowing it, I had already embraced the companionship principle.

The Pressure Is Off

The companionship principle removes a lot of the pressure from dating. I know how it is with the singles in my church: they are afraid to sit next to a guy or girl at church because we'll have them married off by the end of the announcements. Starting with a friendship, though, relieves the pressure—both the well-meaning pressure applied by others and the emotional and sexual pressure dating couples sometimes put on each other.

People date for various reasons; however, the biblical reason to spend time with a guy or a girl is to build a lasting friendship. It might turn into marriage one day; it might not. There's no need to worry about that at the start. And if marriage eventually doesn't appeal to one or the other, nothing has been lost. In fact, a valuable friendship has been forged. That, and the experience they gained building it, will be beneficial for a lifetime.

Playing Games

When dating starts as a friendship, you don't have to pretend to be someone else. The girl doesn't have to play the does-he-really-like-me game. The guy doesn't have to do the knight-in-shining-armor act. The girl doesn't have to worry about how much she will have to give away physically in order to keep his attention.

Consider the average date. You spend three hours with a person doing your absolute best to be someone you aren't. The girl pretends she always looks like she stepped out of a fashion magazine. And the guy—when's the last time he went three hours without burping out loud? On our first date, my wife and I rode bicycles and ate fried chicken—

sweaty faces and greasy fingers. How could a first date survive that? Simple. We had already been friends for a year. We didn't have to play games to impress each other.

A dating relationship guided by the companionship principle of Genesis 2:18 differs radically from what the world promotes. The world tells young people that dating is about romantic emotions and the huggy-kissy game. That totally overlooks the biblical emphasis on pursuing a mutually beneficial friendship.

Been There, Done That?

You know how the typical dating scenario goes. Boy meets girl. Boy asks girl to a movie. They sit in a dark theater for two hours and don't say a word to each other. During the week boy sends girl roses with a note saying her eyes are "sapphire blue."

The next weekend they see another movie. They sit silently for two hours in the dark. This time he holds her hand and steals a kiss on her front steps. The next week it's a necklace instead of flowers and a romantic moonlight walk in the park. They spend half their time trying to suffocate each other (if you know what I mean). And there you have it: they are dating. But is their relationship actually a *friendship*? A mist of emotions and a cloud of lust obscure the lack of any real commitment, sharing, and friendship.

Of course, you know what usually happens in those relationships. In six months their "love" has fallen apart and they break up, only to start over again with someone else a couple of months later. Or, worse yet, they actually get married, and a year or two into marriage they look around and think, "I don't even know this person. And I'm not sure I really enjoy spending time with him or her now that the novelty has worn off."

To bring biblical sanity to those kinds of scenarios, we need to transform our thinking about dating. It starts with Genesis 2:18. Dating is a marriage-kind-of-relationship, and God defined that kind of relationship as *companionship*.

Does this make a difference? Sure it does. For example, apply the companionship principle to physical involvement. Genesis 2:18 immediately calls into question the practice of getting physical in dating. Why would a guy and a girl do that in a *friendship*? Those things are marriage activities, not friendship activities. Based on the companionship principle, I would suggest that many dating relationships should be backed down to the friendship level, and stay there. Dragging in a host of romantic distractions and physical temptations is merely conforming to the world.

Romance and physical affection (of a strictly limited nature) should not come until friendship, commitment, and trust are already well established and marriage is just around the corner. Why take a dating relationship up to the point romantically and physically where marriage is the next step when you can't get married anytime soon? That kind of pressure is a forked road: one branch leads to a painful breakup, the other to sexual sin.

The key to handling dating in a godly way is to let Genesis 2:18 be your guide. If there is someone you're interested in, bury all those romantic notions you've been fed by the world and work on being friends. If your friendship doesn't click, then there is no reason to bother clouding the issue with the frills and thrills of romance and playing around physically. All they do is deceive you into thinking you have a meaningful friendship when you really don't.

3
Where, What, When, and Whom?

Many dating couples want practical advice on where to go and what to do to have fun. To be honest, you probably don't want my help with that. Most people don't consider browsing in used-book stores a cool date.

However, there is one piece of advice I can give you: *do nothing from selfishness.* The biblical basis for that counsel is Paul's letter to the Philippians. Next to Genesis 2:18, I believe Philippians 2:3–4 is the most important biblical guideline for dating. Paul wrote this letter to bring peace and unity to the Philippian church; however, the principles he outlines can also be applied to bringing peace and unity to dating relationships.

> *Do nothing from selfishness or empty conceit, but with humility of mind regard one another as more important than yourselves; do not merely look out for your own personal interests, but also for*

the interests of others.

(Philippians 2:3–4)

Would that be a good description of your dating relationships? Too often, dating is controlled by just the opposite. Our motives are self-centered and vain, and we think primarily of ourselves, not the concerns, interests, and feelings of our "friend."

I remember a situation from high school that illustrates this. Jeff was the best athlete in my school; Jana was the prettiest girl. It was the classic high-school dating relationship. They had been dating for about a year when Jeff decided they should break up. Jeff told Jana at her locker during lunch break. Naturally she was devastated. She cried her way through the next three class periods until school was done for the day.

That's an example of selfishness. The timing of Jeff's announcement was thoughtless and inconsiderate. He didn't regard Jana and her feelings as more important than his own. Had his first thought been for her, he would have told her his decision at a time when her disappointment wouldn't have been a public spectacle.

If you are wondering how to handle anything in a dating friendship, the best counsel I can give you is "Do nothing from selfishness." It might be asking someone out for the first time; it might be planning activities to do together; it might be "breaking up." It doesn't matter. If you "do nothing from selfishness," you will have gone a long way toward handling it rightly. Let me give you four examples to help a bit more.

» *Do nothing from selfishness* won't tell you which restaurant to eat at, but it will tell you whether you should go to a restaurant *you* like or a restaurant *she* likes.

» *Do nothing from empty conceit* doesn't tell you whom to date. But it does tell you that if you're dating a guy because his car and clothes impress your friends, then you are dating with selfish motives. You're not giving to a friendship; you're constructing an image. That's empty conceit.

» *Regard one another as more important than yourselves.* You've probably seen relationships in which the girl (for example) acts as if the guy is her personal property. She pressures him to order his life so that she is at the center of it. She isn't regarding him as more important than herself: clearly she thinks that she is the more important person in the relationship.

» *Do not merely look out for your own personal interests* ... "I need you. I love you. I can't live without you." When a guy says things like that to pressure his girlfriend to keep the relationship going, is he looking out for her best interests? Certainly not. His words prove that the only one he loves in that relationship is himself.

The applications of Philippians 2:3–4 to dating are endless. One way or another, these verses will guide every word, decision, and action in your friendship.

Let's move to another question: Whom can I date? The world emphasizes what she looks like or how prestigious he is in the eyes of your friends. Applying the companionship principle of Genesis 2:18 allows us to throw out all those peripheral things. The real questions are: Can I be a good friend to him or her? Will our friendship be mutually profitable and enjoyable?

Let's examine five important considerations regarding whom to date.

1. What Is His or Her Spiritual Condition?

When answering the question "Whom can I date?" the first consideration is the other person's spiritual condition. If you are a Christian, it is impossible to have a spiritually profitable relationship with someone who is not a Christian. First Corinthians 7:39 helps you know how to handle a marriage-kind-of-relationship because it lays down an absolute rule about marriage itself:

> *A wife is bound as long as her husband lives; but if her husband is dead, she is free to be married to whom she wishes, only in the Lord.*

A Christian is to marry *only in the Lord*. "But that's talking about marriage," you complain. Yes, but why would you consider pursuing a *marriage-kind-of-relationship* with someone God says you *can't* marry? Why start down that disastrous path? Why suffer the emotional agony of having to extricate yourself from that relationship later on? Worse yet, you might never come to your senses. Then you will be destined to a lifetime of spiritual solitaire, and there is nothing more lonely than a spiritually unequal marriage. First

Corinthians 7:39 and the companionship principle team up to deliver a clear message: as a believer in Jesus Christ, don't even consider dating a person who is not a Christian.

You might ask, "How do I know if someone is a Christian? How do I know if *I* am a Christian? We often use the word "Christian" in a cultural sense—Christian in contrast to Hindu, Moslem, or Jew. That's not what I'm referring to when I say that you should pursue a marriage-kind-of-relationship only with another Christian.

To be a Christian in the true sense of the word is to believe in Jesus Christ. By that I don't mean some kind of vague, general, Sunday-school belief. Christianity is about Jesus Christ, the God-man, dying for sinners on the cross. Why did he do that? In those awful hours of physical and spiritual suffering, Jesus took the punishment for sin that you and I deserve. Three days later, God raised Jesus from the dead to declare that Christ's work on the cross was complete and acceptable. Why was this necessary? Because God is holy and just, and he cannot overlook evil. Therefore, although sinless himself, Jesus willingly took on himself all the Father's wrath against our wrongdoing. The one who believes in Jesus as his or her substitute, bearing God's wrath in his or her place, and seeks

God's forgiveness on that basis alone is a Christian.

Saving faith is a humble submission to Christ as both gracious Savior and authoritative Lord:

> *If you confess with your mouth Jesus as Lord, and believe in your heart that God raised Him from the dead, you will be saved.*
>
> (Romans 10:9)

In short, if this is true of you, then you have been redeemed by Jesus Christ, and should date or marry only someone who has a true, submissive faith in Christ as well.

2. What is His or Her Spiritual-Interest Level?

Dating an unbeliever is clearly off-limits; however, the companionship principle warns you against something else as well: beware of dating a professing believer whose level of spiritual interest is markedly lower than yours. Companionship means shared interests, especially a mutual love for Jesus Christ. If the person you're interested in professes Christ but lags behind in actual spiritual interest and activity, reconsider. You will never find true companionship with him or her.

A friend of mine once said, "I love Jim and I want to marry him, but he just doesn't lead our relationship spiritually. I think he's saved, but he doesn't have the same desire for Christ, God's Word, and serving in the church that I do. If I marry him, I'll end up growing backwards spiritually." The problem was so obvious that my friend was willing to call off her relationship with Jim completely. She was wise. Marrying someone who has little or no spiritual interest will drain your spiritual vitality dry. Whatever else is desirable in a relationship, never settle for second-rate spiritual companionship.

3. Is He or She a Fool?

Pursuing a marriage-kind-of-relationship with a fool is dooming yourself to misery and harm:

> He who walks with wise men will be wise,
> But the companion of fools will suffer
>   harm.
>
>   (Proverbs 13:20)

But how can you know if the guy or girl you're interested in is someone God would call a fool?

Let me give you a list of verses that will help:

- "He who conceals hatred has lying lips, and he who spreads slander is a fool" (Proverbs 10:18). A fool tells lies and spreads slander, saying untrue or hurtful things to protect him- or herself or to get at others. If the person you are interested in has a lying or abrasive tongue, scratch him or her off your list immediately.

- "The way of a fool is right in his own eyes, but a wise man is he who listens to counsel" (Proverbs 12:15). The fool is conceited, always thinking he or she is right. Thus, this person refuses to be corrected. Who wants to pursue a marriage-kind-of-relationship with someone who refuses to admit he or she is wrong?

- "A wise son makes a father glad, but a foolish man despises his mother" (Proverbs 15:20). Fools often have bad relationships with their parents. If someone speaks disrespectfully to or about his or her parents (or treats them badly in any other way), stay away. How this person treats his or her family reveals how he or she will treat you once the facade of dating politeness is dropped.

- "A fool's lips bring strife, and his mouth calls for blows" (Proverbs 18:6). Have you noticed an increased level of conflict with your family and friends since you started dating someone? Is he or she often the vortex of those conflicts? Maybe you are dating a fool, because fools are always surrounded by a thundercloud of strife.
- "The fool folds his hands and consumes his own flesh" (Ecclesiastes 4:5). The "folding hands" terminology connects this to the sluggard of Proverbs (6:6–11; 24:30–34). If a guy has never held a job, doesn't carry through on responsibilities, or doesn't work consistently before marriage, then he won't afterwards, either. Walking up an aisle, mumbling "I do," and then walking back down the aisle doesn't transform a person's character.
- "Keeping away from strife is an honor for a man, but any fool will quarrel" (Proverbs 20:3). A fool often quarrels. Why would you want that in a companion?
- "A fool always loses his temper, but a wise man holds it back" (Proverbs 29:11). Don't kid yourself; eventually you will be the target of your boyfriend's or girlfriend's anger.

Don't let some good points blind your eyes to a person's lack of true commitment to Jesus Christ. If you find yourself continually excusing your boyfriend's or girlfriend's behavior, it could be that he or she is a fool. Call sin "sin," and call off the relationship. In short, follow Solomon's instruction:

> *Leave the presence of a fool.*
> (Proverbs 14:7)

4. Am I Old Enough?

"When can I start dating?" That's a question that should spark some controversy! Depending on whether you ask teenagers or their parents, the answer will be either thirteen or thirty-nine.

Let's start with young adults. You may not know it, but there is a verse in the Bible that tells you exactly when you can start dating. It pinpoints it down to the *day*. That relieves a lot of pressure, doesn't it? No arguments with Dad and Mom— just let the Bible tell us. Are you ready? Here is the verse:

> *Children, obey your parents in the Lord,*

for this is right. Honor your father and mother ...

(Ephesians 6:1–2)

Okay, so you hate me. I know. But that's what it says. For the young adult, this issue is easy: honor whatever your father and mother decide. They are your God-given protectors to rescue you from the foolishness bound up in your heart. You can be glad they are looking out for you.

For parents, the issue is a little more complex. There is no Bible verse that says when a young adult should be allowed to date. But don't despair. When in doubt about dating, go back to Genesis 2:18 and the companionship principle. If you take the huggy-kissy thing and the emotional bungee-jumping out of it, is there any problem with your child cultivating friendships with spiritually alive members of the opposite sex? I don't think so. You are, however, going to have to help your young adult understand what friendship is. You'll need to help him or her avoid drowning in an emotional flood. You need to provide an environment where there is no opportunity to get involved physically.

The parents' responsibility is to train their children to be ready to "leave ... father and mother" for a marriage relationship (Genesis 2:24). Therefore, if you are a parent, be diligent in teaching your kids about godly friendship. You may choose never to let your children date, as the world practices it, while they are in your home. But you must teach them to value companionship and to avoid emotional and physical pitfalls in their friendships with the opposite sex.

5. What Will We Live On?

"You can't live on love!" How many young couples who want to get married have heard that? It makes the prospective couple grind their teeth, but finances are a legitimate issue—not just in regard to marriage, but also in regard to dating. It pains me to see sixteen-year-olds hanging onto each other like newlyweds. A sixteen-year-old can't provide a living for a family; therefore, there is no place for that relationship to go. It is foolish to take a relationship to the brink of marriage physically and emotionally when marriage is not an option financially.

I don't mean that you have to have a car, a house, and your career all sorted out before you think about marriage. However, I do believe, if you are pursuing a serious marriage-kind-of-relationship, the guy had better be able to provide a realistic minimum income should things work out. Otherwise you are left in a relationship with a very high level of intimacy, but no outlet. Who wants to live with that kind of frustration?

It is much wiser to keep that relationship at the friendship level until marriage is an option financially. If you are in college, that might mean working on a friendship until graduation. Or it might mean re-ordering life so that you can get married, work to meet your family's needs, and attend classes on a part-time basis.

That second option runs against the thinking of our culture, but I find nothing especially biblical about interminably delaying marriage in order to pile up educational and career achievements. Genesis 2:18 doesn't say anything about a degree or a career, but it does make it clear that those whom God has gifted to be married will usually function better if they are.

4
Purity and Dating

A young woman once told me that she was shocked to discover that virtually all her friends in her college youth group were sleeping with their boyfriends. Unfortunately, that sort of thing is all too common. You've heard all the excuses: "We're going to get married anyway," or "We thought we could stop before it went this far." God, however, calls Christians to live differently.

> For this is the will of God, your sanctification; that is, that you abstain from sexual immorality.
>
> (1 Thessalonians 4:3)

"Sexual immorality" refers to any sexual activity outside of marriage. Within marriage, sex is a pure and delightful gift from God. However, any sexual activity before marriage or outside of marriage after the wedding is a perversion of God's good gift. Therefore, every Christian dating couple needs to make purity its goal.

Purity and Dating

The world often encourages young people to turn the burner of physical involvement on high. A non-Christian friend once complained to me that a girl was cold because she wouldn't give him a goodnight kiss on their first date. It's not surprising he thought that way. Our culture furiously promotes sexual immorality. By the time he or she is twenty, the average person in our culture has seen immorality sensually acted out on television or in movies hundreds of times. And the outside pressure from the culture is nothing compared with the internal pressure of our own desires. How can dating couples avoid the temptation of playing around physically? Let's find the answer by looking at four principles from Proverbs.

1. Remember Your Divine Accountability

Why should you, my son, be exhilarated
  with an adulteress,
And embrace the bosom of a foreigner?

For the ways of a man are before the eyes
  of the LORD,
And He watches all his paths.
                              (Proverbs 5:20–21)

Why did Solomon tell his son to avoid going astray with an adulteress? Because "the ways of a man are before the eyes of the LORD." The couple that mess around when their parents are out, or when they're alone at her apartment, think that no one knows what they are doing. In contrast, Proverbs says that their sensual acts are committed in bright daylight at the foot of the throne of God. Remembering that God always knows exactly what you are doing is a compelling motivation to keep your dating relationships pure.

2. Maintain Human Accountability

If you fail to restrain yourself, you'll end up like the immoral fool in Proverbs 5:12–13, lamenting,

> ... *How I have hated instruction!*
>   *And my heart spurned reproof!*
> *I have not listened to the voice of my*
>   *teachers,*
>   *Nor inclined my ear to my instructors.*

Those cries of regret highlight the usefulness of human teachers. We are accountable to God, but sometimes our hormone-seared consciences are deaf to God's promptings. It helps to have someone directly in front of you who can look you in the eye and say, "Don't do that. Avoid that situation." Furthermore, if you know you'll have to tell your parents or another spiritual advisor the nature of your physical relationship with your boyfriend or girlfriend that week, you'll be much more likely to exercise self-control. Humble your pride, be accountable, and stay pure.

3. Consider the Consequences of Failing to Exercise Self-Control

> Can a man take fire in his bosom,
>   And his clothes not be burned?
> Or can a man walk on hot coals,
>   And his feet not be scorched?
> So is the one who goes in to his neighbor's wife;
>   Whoever touches her will not go unpunished.
>
> (Proverbs 6:27–29)

When a dating couple are getting hot and heavy on the couch, they aren't thinking about the consequences of their sin: the shame of being caught, the guilt if they aren't. But that is typical of sexual lust; it is heedless of consequences.

Speaking of the adulteress, Solomon says,

> *She does not ponder the path of life;*
> *Her ways are unstable, she does not know it.*
>
> (Proverbs 5:6)

Proverbs speaks of the devastating results of taking your foot off the brake pedal when it comes to self-control. It warns of enslavement to lust, a seared conscience, blackmail, illegitimate pregnancy, the financial drain of child support, sexually transmitted diseases, public shame, bitterness, anger, and incapacitating guilt (see Proverbs 5:7–14).

The powerful temptation and hidden consequences of sexual sin are expressed perfectly by Solomon in Proverbs 5:3–5:

> *For the lips of an adulteress drip honey,*
> *And smoother than oil is her speech;*
> *But in the end she is bitter as wormwood,*
> *Sharp as a two-edged sword.*
> *Her feet go down to death,*
> *Her steps take hold of Sheol [the grave].*

Although pleasing God is the most important

reason for staying pure, the consequences of sexual sin are also a key motivation not to play with fire when it comes to sexual purity.

4. Do Not Go Near the Door of Sexual Temptation

> *Now then, my sons, listen to me,*
>   *And do not depart from the words of my mouth.*
> *Keep your way far from her [the adulteress],*
>   *And do not go near the door of her house.*
> (Proverbs 5:7–8)

You can avoid a lot of sin just by avoiding the opportunity. Copy Joseph: when temptation reaches out to grab you, put on your track spikes and get out of there (Genesis 39:7–12). In fact, even better is never getting within arm's reach of sexual temptation. In other words, the best way to flee youthful lusts is to completely avoid situations where you'll have an opportunity to get in trouble.

THE SEDUCTION

To illustrate the importance of not going near the door of sexual temptation, Solomon does a very interesting thing in Proverbs 7. He gives us a movie script or a one-act play that I call *The Seduction*. It shows how someone can fall (or walk open-eyed) into sexual sin. There are two characters in the play: a foolish young man and a loose-living woman. We meet the foolish young man first.

> *And I saw among the naive,*
>   *And discerned among the youths,*
>   *A young man lacking sense,*
> *Passing through the street near her corner;*
>   *And he takes the way to her house,*
> *In the twilight, in the evening,*
>   *In the middle of the night and in the darkness.*
>
> (Proverbs 7:7–9)

A young man passing through the streets at evening seems innocent enough, but the narrator informs us that he has an aim to his walking. The verb Solomon used means the young man "stepped with a cadence." He was marching quickly, with a purposeful stride. He wasn't *planning* to stop at the adulteress's house; in fact, according to 7:13, he had to be persuaded to enter. Nonetheless, his intent was to walk by her house to see what would happen.

Like many dating couples who struggle with

sexual temptation, this young man wasn't planning to sin. But he wasn't planning *not to sin*, either. He didn't go straight to the adulteress's house and bang on her door; he was just innocently walking by. But the truth of the matter is that he was making himself available for immoral activity if the opportunity arose. The nervous excitement in his steps is a dead giveaway.

And notice *when* he walked by: after dark (v. 9). He was flirting with sexual temptation at a time when he knew no one would see him, when his activity would be hidden, when he would not be interrupted (see vv. 18-20). He wasn't planning to sin, but he was constructing a situation in which he would have every opportunity to sin without being caught.

Sound familiar? Christian dating couples rarely *plan* to commit sexual sin. But how often do they put themselves in situations where the opportunity to sin is available? Knowingly giving themselves undue opportunity to live out their fantasies, they later foolishly lament, "We never planned for this, we never expected it to go this far."

Sometimes dating or engaged couples say to me, "We're struggling to maintain purity in our relationship. Will you help us?" I always ask them, "When do you struggle most?" Typical answer:

"When we're watching romantic movies on the couch late at night when our parents or roommates aren't home." I think we found the problem! They aren't necessarily planning to sin, but they sure aren't planning to avoid it either.

I used the word "fantasies" above. Proverbs also warns about the dangerous role daydreams play in sexual temptation. As you read the next verse, keep in mind that, in the Bible, the word "heart" refers to your thinking, and, in this case, especially to your imagination:

> Do not let your heart [imagination] turn
>   aside to her ways,
> Do not stray into her paths.
> (Proverbs 7:25)

If you daydream about kissing, touching, and other sensual activities, you're walking right up to the doorway of sexual temptation.

When you're dating, plan to be together in places where you'll have accountability. If you want to be alone at times, that's fine. You should, however, plan to be alone in public places—a park, a restaurant, or something like that. A distant bedroom with the door closed is not the place to spend time together. That's a recipe for disaster.

Purity and Dating

Unfortunately, like many dating couples, the young man in *The Seduction* hadn't given a second's thought to avoiding sexual sin; therefore, his downfall was virtually determined. And, in this case, the girl wasn't helping.

DRESSED TO KILL

*And behold, a woman comes to meet him,
Dressed as a harlot ...*

(Proverbs 7:10)

A young woman can contribute to the ongoing purity of a dating friendship by taking care how she dresses. Every woman wants to look attractive—there's nothing necessarily wrong with that. But through magazines and movies our culture bombards her with the notion that the more of her body she shows, the better she looks.

Adding to the problem is the fact that many young women have little idea of the extent to which their clothing (or lack thereof) affects men. What a young woman thinks is fashionable might be sending a different message altogether to men: "My body is available. Look and see."

I had a friend in college who said that, when she was in high school, her brothers acted as her inspectors every morning. When she came down the stairs for school in a new outfit, sometimes they just shook their heads and pointed back up the stairs. They wouldn't let her out the door until she changed. As you can imagine, it frustrated her immensely, but as she looked back, she valued their policing: they were protecting her and her reputation. They understood, even if she didn't, that her clothes sent a message.

I knew her for three years. She was a pretty girl who received a lot of attention from the guys, but I can't recall one time seeing her dressed in something questionable. Her brothers had taught her well. As young men, we all respected her: she was a godly young lady and was to be treated as such. The way she dressed made it clear.

"I Have Nothing to Wear!"

Right now, you girls might be asking, "Do I have to throw out my whole wardrobe? What is appropriate dress? I don't want to lead men to think sinful thoughts!" Knowing how men think, the legalist in me would like to say, "Ankles, wrists, and earlobes—everything else must be covered!" But seriously, here is the test I use for my wife. It doesn't even require a tape measure. I call it the "preposition test." If you can see *up* it, *down* it, or *through* it, then dump it. No matter how stylish the world says it is, get rid of it.

If you have to pull it down or super-glue your knees together to keep someone from seeing up it, if you have to pull it closed to keep someone from looking down it, if it has to be at least ninety-five degrees in the shade to wear it, or if it looks like it was put on with an airbrush, then I can guarantee it is inappropriate.

Some women's fashions look as if the seamstress ran out of material halfway through the pattern. Others are so tight that, while they cover everything, they also reveal everything. Don't capitulate to the world when it comes to standards of modesty. The question is not, "How much can I show?" The question is, "How far will I go to make sure I am not unintentionally advertising my body?" Save your body for your husband's eyes. That's an attitude that God values and men respect. It will also help your date keep his mind on your friendship, rather than having to avert his eyes every time you cross your legs or lean forward.

Frogs and Princes

We're still working on our fourth principle of dating purity: *don't go near the door of sexual temptation*. We find another point of application in Proverbs 7:10–13:

> *And behold, a woman comes to meet him...*
> *... She seizes him and kisses him.*
>   (Proverbs 7:10, 13a)

How did the actual enticement of the young fool begin? With a kiss. A kiss can be a relatively harmless thing; in many cultures it is a standard form of greeting. But that's not what this text is talking about. Verse 13 says she *seized* him: she grabbed him in a passionate embrace and kissed him provocatively.

If friendship is the biblical idea behind dating, then where does this come in? Does the girl hope that the frog she is dating will turn into a prince if she kisses him? Does he have such a dull personality that he has to kiss her to wake his sleeping beauty? Seriously, the seductress in Proverbs 7 used her kiss as *a promise of greater pleasure to come.* That's what touching and passionate kissing do: they set off physiological processes that are extremely difficult to suppress or stop.

If you are doing that to your date, you're betraying him or her. If your expressions of physical affection are making it difficult for your "friend" to restrain the progress of his or her natural physical desires, then you are acting just like the seductress in Proverbs 7. Regardless of your intentions, you are enticing another to sexual sin; you are promising what you cannot (or should not) deliver until marriage.

The temptation to play around is strong, but these four principles from Proverbs will go a long way toward guarding your purity.

Conclusion: Is This the One?

When I saw my wife for the first time, I was dumbstruck. She didn't walk, she floated down the steps from her second-floor office and passed me with a dazzling smile. I choked out a greeting of some kind and then collapsed weakly against a convenient wall, exhausted by the effort. A few days later I told my best friend that I had met the girl I was going to marry. Being the objective type, he asked me, "What do you mean by that?"

"I mean, she is gorgeous, *and* if I find out her name, *and* if we get to know each other, *and* she loves the Lord, *and* we develop a godly friendship, *and* our parents and spiritual leaders approve ..." Well, you get the point. My friend was right to be concerned: deciding whom to marry needs to be based on a lot more than sparkling eyes and a radiant smile. Therefore, the last question I want to deal with is this: How do I know if he or she is

Conclusion: Is This the One?

the one for me?

There has probably been more nonsense propagated about this than about anything else in dating: "You'll just *know* she's the one." But what if *he* knows she's the one, but *she* doesn't? How do you make sure—lift a tag at the back and see if your name is on it? "If you *really* love him, then he's the one." But what is the difference between kind-of-love and real love? Does a flaming heart descend from heaven and touch you both on the forehead? Do you glow in the dark? Do you hear violin music whenever you are together?

The mystical ways people decide whom to marry (inner voices or outward signs) are among the things that create insanity in dating. In their place, let me give you six basic, practical questions to ask yourself as you determine whether the person you are spending time with is "the right one." Ask these questions within a lifestyle of prayerful dependence on God, for the Bible clearly emphasizes the priority of prayer in the life of the Christian. For example, Paul commanded the Thessalonians, "Pray without ceasing" (1 Thessalonians 5:17), and Jesus instructed his disciples that "at all times they ought to pray and not to lose heart" (Luke 18:1).

1. What Do Your Parents Say?

Don't pull a Samson and ignore your parents' counsel. They are your God-given protectors. Believers or not, their perspective on your relationship is critical. Parents also have a way of bringing a young couple back to earth with questions about finances and other items of a practical nature. That's a good thing.

2. What Do Your Spiritual Leaders Think?

Hebrews 13:17 says that church leaders are there to "keep watch over your souls"; therefore, make sure they have an opportunity to shepherd you in regard to choosing a life partner. As spiritual leaders, they should be wise and insightful; therefore, they might discern spiritual issues in your relationship that you are overlooking. They might have doubts about the salvation or spiritual maturity of your prospective partner. It is equally likely that they will be enthusiastic about your relationship. Whatever the case, their counsel should be sought and heeded.

3. What Do Your Spiritually Minded Friends Think?

Years ago I had a friend who was dating a girl who was the personification of the contentious woman in the book of Proverbs. In public she was polite and refined; in private she was bitter and bossy. When they started to talk about marriage, his closest friends sat him down and encouraged him from Scripture not to marry her. He chose to ignore their counsel, and three years later he had to drop out of seminary because his marriage was in such turmoil. They had fooled their parents and church leaders because they saw the two of them only in public. But his room-mates saw them together every day, and they knew what their relationship was really like.

Although spiritually minded friends don't have the same authority as parents and spiritual leaders, they might know your relationship better. Therefore, their honest, biblical appraisal of your relationship is valuable. However, beware of friends who tell you only what you want to hear or who don't have biblical standards. They might do more harm than good.

When I was dating my wife, it was critical to me that my parents, spiritual leaders, and spiritually minded friends gave me an honest evaluation of our relationship. I knew that my eyes were blinded by emotional intoxication. Had any of those three groups had a problem with our relationship, I would have put the brakes on the relationship immediately.

4. Are the Basic Commands Regarding Marriage in Ephesians 5:22–33 Working Relatively Smoothly?

In other words, as the man, are you leading the relationship, and is your leadership typified by sacrificial love? As the woman, are you respectfully submitting to his leadership? Can you see yourself doing so for the rest of your life?

Dating is not marriage. A girl is not required to "submit" to her boyfriend's authority. However, if biblical leadership and submission are not developing as the relationship progresses, then a couple should be very wary of getting married. Sacrificial love and gracious submission are *the* biblical commands regarding marriage. If they are not functioning at an effective level, then marriage is going to be a very rough haul indeed.

Don't marry someone for what you hope he or she will be. Get married on the basis of who the

Conclusion: Is This the One?

person currently is and what your relationship currently is. Marrying hopes is a dangerous proposition.

5. Is He or She Interested in Marrying You?

That's kind of important, isn't it? I can hear you moaning right now, "But how do I know if he or she is interested?" It's simpler than you think: talk about it. "But," says the guy, "how can I talk to her about *that*?" Well, you're friends, aren't you? If you can't talk openly about serious matters concerning your relationship, then maybe you don't have the kind of friendship you thought you did.

Friendship takes all the game-playing out of dating. Just be honest: "I really enjoy our relationship. If things continue to go this way, I would like to think about the possibility of marriage some day. What do you think?" She might say, "I'm not sure I'm ready to think about that yet." Then you say, "Okay, I won't pressure you about it. Let's just continue to enjoy being friends."

If, however, she says, "I'm interested. Keep talking," then go have pizza and talk about marriage and see if your ideas mesh. By not popping the question out of the blue, you are considering the other person as more important than yourself. Patience, honesty, and openness have always been the hallmarks of a good friendship. I have no idea why we set that aside when we contemplate engagement and marriage.

Sometimes I hear girls exclaim, "I never expected him to ask me to marry him!" When I hear that, I think, "And you said *yes*? You are going to order your whole earthly life based on an emotional whim? Don't you think you should talk about it before you give your word to him?" When considering whether you want to marry someone you are dating, it's important to know if he or she wants to marry you. Be open. Talk about it. If your friendship isn't ready for that, it's not strong enough to be the basis of a marriage anyway.

6. Do You Want to Marry Him or Her?

If all the other questions have been asked and answered satisfactorily, and you want to marry the person, then my counsel is, "Go for it." "But what if it's not God's will?" I suspect that if all the other factors line up, and you want to marry the person, God has no problem with it. Pray for wisdom, but don't get caught up in mystical methods of

Conclusion: Is This the One?

decision-making when it comes to marriage.

Those six questions make deciding whom to marry a lot more objective. They force you to see your relationship as it really is. They seek and honor God's wisdom through parents and mature spiritual advisors. That kind of straight, biblical thinking is the basis of good decision-making for marriage and everything else.

In summary, starting with the companionship principle in Genesis 2:18 helps remove the confusion that the world has injected into dating. God is honored by selfless friendships. Once you find a companion who is too good to lose, and your friendship has developed in trust, commitment, and selflessness, ask and answer the six questions listed above. Then, if your answers are positive, enjoy God's gift of a Christ-centered companionship for a lifetime.

In the meantime, I'm sure things will go better for you than they did on my first date. How could it get worse than that? Well, actually it can get worse. Someday I'll tell you about my second date. But until then, remember that dating can be biblical. It can be pure. It can be enjoyable. If you work hard at loving Christ and applying his Word, it will be all those things and more.

Personal Application Projects

1. Look up the following verses in Proverbs and write down the character qualities you should exhibit if you're a man or you should look for in a potential mate if you're a woman: Proverbs 10:26; 11:25; 14:17; 16:19; 19:22; 20:6; 22:24–25; 26:21; 29:23.

2. The contentious woman is one of the anti-heroes of Proverbs. From the verses below, note her character qualities and their God-honoring replacements. If you are a young man, how should these verses shape what you look for in a potential wife? If you are a woman, what adjustments to your own life should you make in light of these Scriptures? Proverbs 1:9; 21:19; 27:15–16, 14:1; 9:13; 12:4; 11:22; 31:30.

3. Read Romans 13:14. What two commands does God give in this verse? List eight specific practical things you can do to limit your opportunities to fall into sexual impurity while dating. Next, read the following verses

Help! I'm Confused about Dating

to see how a love for Jesus Christ can keep you from pushing the line of purity: John 3:2–3; John 5:3; John 14:15.

4. Sometimes it's hard to take the advice of your parents or other spiritual advisors when it comes to dating. Read the following verses and note what Proverbs says about receiving counsel. How does this apply to you? Proverbs 9:7–9; 10:17; 12:15; 15:12; 17:10; 26:12; 27:22; 28:26; 29:1.

5. Godly character is essential to a good dating relationship. Read the following verses from Proverbs and write down the key character qualities you should be building in yourself and be looking for in someone you date: Proverbs 9:10; 11:13; 12:19; 15:1; 16:32; 18:2; 23:4–5; 23:20–21; 27:4; 28:6; 29:25.

6. Make a list of the virtues that contribute to a good friendship. One is unselfishness. Read Philippians 2:3–8 to see how Jesus is the ultimate example of selflessness. Also note Paul and Timothy's examples of selflessness in Philippians 1:21–25; 2:19–22; 4:10, 15–17.

7. A good friendship includes at least the following characteristics: sacrifice, forgiveness, listening, loyalty, respect,

peace, spiritual fellowship, love, serving, and spiritual refreshment. Match each of these characteristics with the verse below that most clearly teaches it: Romans 12:18; Proverbs 18:13; Philemon 7; John 15:13; 1 Samuel 18:1; Ephesians 4:32; Proverbs 27:10; Romans 12:10b; Psalm 34:3; John 13:12–15.

Where Can I Get More Help?

Baucham, Voddie, *What He Must Be ... if He Wants to Marry My Daughter* (Wheaton, IL: Crossway, 2009)

James, Joel, *Biblical Decision-Making: Is it God's Will to Find His Will?* (2001; booklet available to download under "Resources" at www.gracefellowship.co.za)

Philips, Richard and Sharon, *Holding Hands, Holding Hearts* (Phillipsburg, NJ: P&R, 2006)

BOOKS IN THE HELP! SERIES INCLUDE...

- Help! He's Struggling with Pornography
- Help! Someone I Love Has Been Abused
- Help! My Toddler Rules the House
- Help! Someone I Love Has Cancer
- Help! I Want to Change
- Help! My Spouse Has Been Unfaithful
- Help! Someone I Love Has Alzheimer's
- Help! I Have Breast Cancer
- Help! I'm a Slave to Food
- Help! My Teen Struggles With Same-Sex Attractions
- Help! She's Struggling With Pornography
- Help! I Can't Get Motivated
- Help! I'm a Single Mom
- Help! I'm Confused About Dating
- Help! I'm Drowning in Debt
- Help! My Teen is Rebellious
- Help! I'm Depressed
- Help! I'm Living With Terminal Illness
- Help! I Feel Ashamed
- Help! I Want to Model Submission in Marriage
- Help! I Can't Handle All These Trials
- Help! I Can't Forgive
- Help! My Anger is Out of Control
- Help! My Friend is Suicidal
- Help! I'm in a Conflict
- Help! I'm Being Deployed
- Help! I've Been Traumatized by Combat
- Help! I'm So Lonely
- Help! My Kids Are Viewing Porn
- Help! I Need a Church

More titles in preparation

For current listing visit www.shepherdpress.com/lifeline

About Shepherd Press Publications

» They are gospel driven.
» They are heart focused.
» They are life changing.

Our Invitation to You

We passionately believe that what we are publishing can be of benefit to you, your family, your friends, and your work colleagues. So we are inviting you to join our online mailing list so that we may reach out to you with news about our latest and forthcoming publications, and with special offers.

Visit:

www.shepherdpress.com/newsletter
and provide your name and email address.